SOCCER RULES
for
SUCCESS IN BUSINESS

Brendan B. Michael

© Brendan B. Michael 2021

All rights reserved. No part of this publication may be reproduced, stored in a retrieval system, or transmitted in any form or by any means, electronic, mechanical, photocopying, recording or otherwise, without the prior written permission of the copyright owner.

ISBN: 9798508374730

Published By: McBrandon Publishers
A Division of:
McBrandon Business Consulting
1, Olukoya Street,
Felele Rab,
Ibadan, Nigeria.
Tel.: +2348135830704, +2348030655262, +2349059371424.
E-mail: mcbrandonbc@gmail.com

www.mcbrandon-business-consulting.com.ng

For enquiries, contact:

Business Ideas Hub (BizIHub)

- bizihub.com.ng@gmail.com   https://www.facebook.com/bizihub
  Tel.: +234 809 911 3414

- www.bizihub.com.ng

Contents

Contents

Content		iii
Dedication		iv
Acknowledgement		v
Chapter One:	Introduction	7
Chapter Two:	Rule of Fit	11
Chapter Three:	Rule of Replacement	17
Chapter Four:	Rule of Fair Play	23
Chapter Five:	Rule of Reward	29
Chapter Six:	Rule of Timing	37
Chapter Seven:	Rule of Recess	43
Chapter Eight:	Rule of Training	47
Chapter Nine:	Rule of Differentiation	53
Chapter Ten:	Rule of Penalty	57
Chapter Eleven:	Rule of Whistle Blowing	63
Chapter Twelve:	Summary	69
Chapter Thirteen:	Conclusion	73
Image/Hypertext Index		74
Note		76

DEDICATION

This book is dedicated to every entrepreneur around the world whose decisions have helped to build lives, industries, economies of nations and of the world at large. Also, to every dedicated team player in different industries around the world whose contribution has helped (and still is helping) to improve lives, industries, economies of nations and of the world.

ACKNOWLEDGMENTS

The success of this book is not unconnected with God's grace and favour. I can't just thank God enough for His love.

Special thanks to Christianah and Joanna Michael for their support and understanding especially during the writing stage of this book.

To my mentor and former employer – Dr. (Mrs.) Omolara Smith, the Medical Director of Molly Specialist Hospital, Ibadan, Oyo State, Nigeria, I will say that I was privileged to have been trained and supervised by you.

To Dr. Tor Terry Shaguy, I draw much strength and inspiration from your books. Thank you.

But for my encounter with Rev'd S. T. Olawale, I would not have harnessed my writing capability and this piece of writing would not have been published at this time or perhaps, it may never have been published at all.

To my friends and colleagues, I thank you for your encouragements. I am particularly indebted to Deacon Babajide Fadipe whose encouraging words are like fuel for my fire. Thank you.

CHAPTER ONE
INTRODUCTION

There are many types of games but basically, we have two forms of games – indoor and outdoor. While the former is played within a small enclosed area away from interference of the weather (rain, wind, sun, etc); the latter is played outside in a larger play area, say, a field, a court, a course or even a much larger land area. People who enjoy their favorite games or who have found them interesting would agree that what make these games interesting and enjoyable are the rules guiding the games. You play every game according to the rules guiding such a game in order to enjoy it..

In any game, there are rules guiding its successful operation. Without these rules, the games will be lopsided, confusing and uninteresting. Imagine that in a game of football, there are no rules against infringement, say, there is no provision for issuance of yellow cards against any player for aggressiveness or a premeditated violent act, the entire field of play could turn to a battle field before ninety minutes of play time.

In football game, for example, there is universality of rules. There are defined play areas, outside of which, the ball should not go in the course of a game. If a ball goes outside the defined football pitch, the referee calls for a throw-in, a corner kick or a goal kick, depending on the situation.

Like the football, there must be universality of rules guiding any business whether it is a small, medium scale or a big business. Without these rules, a business may not operate successfully. It is the correct application of these rules that will help any business to weather the storm of the business environment, especially, the external environmental factors; including: Political, Economic, Social, Technological, Legal and Environmental.

In the wake of the dreaded Corona Virus Disease (COVID-19) pandemic which started in most part of the world sometime around January 2020, a great number of businesses suffered untold hardship while some went into complete bankruptcy as a result of their inability to weather the business storm.

We all saw the industries that were the most hit and some that were moderately hit. We also saw some businesses that enjoyed skyrocketing profits during the pandemic just as much as we saw new businesses springing up even in the complete lockdown period.

One of the most hit sectors was education. The school system suffered a great blow by the COVID-19 pandemic. Most private school proprietors could not afford to pay full salaries to their workers. Many of the most hit private school proprietors could not even afford to pay any salaries to their staff. They could not pay because they were not prepared for any surge in unfavourable or unfriendly external environmental factors.

In my interactions with a number of private school proprietors last year, I discovered that some of them do not run their schools as a going concern but rather, as a cash cow. They take as much profit as they desire to cater for their personal needs like buying private cars, building good houses for themselves, sending their children to better schools and so on. They refuse to take care of their cash cows until these cows grow lean and are unable to produce enough milk.

I observed that they do not operate their schools as profit centres or as strategic business units for the branches. A profit centre is an organization with assignable revenues and costs that operates with a purpose of producing profits. A strategic business unit (SBU) is an autonomous division of a larger company or business that has assignable costs and should necessarily produce a profit or a loss as the case may be. If, as a private school owner, or an entrepreneur, you fail to establish your business cost and to define the revenue that can both absorb the cost and produce a profit; then you are not running your school or business as a profit centre or as a strategic business unit.

For your business to stay afloat at all times, you need to operate within some defined standard business rules. These rules shall be discussed in the following chapters:

CHAPTER TWO
RULE OF FIT

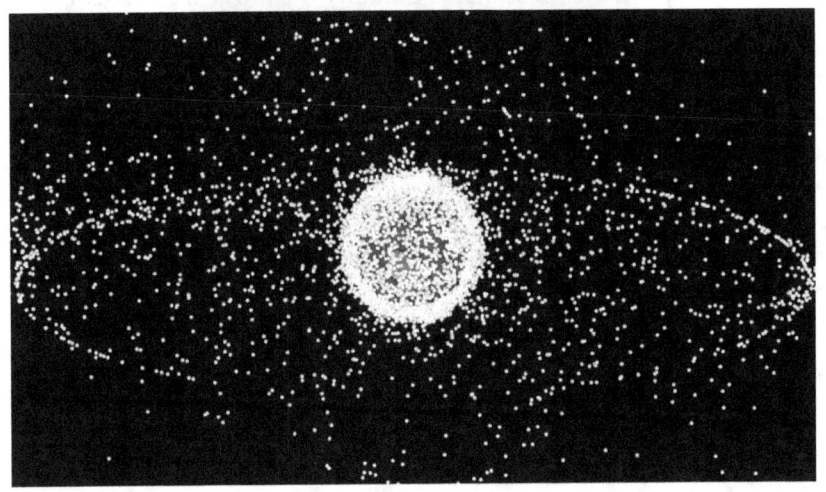

© The World

In the game of football, a match is played by two teams, each with a maximum of eleven players. Have you ever thought why there are eleven players in a football team and five players in a basketball team? Why are there not nine or even seven players in a football team? The inventors of these games just thought of an imaginary number and felt that the number should be adequate for a standard field of play. Does it then mean that, with any given number less than eleven in a team, a football game cannot be played? 'No'.

People play football in smaller pitches in their villages, on the streets and even in their small backyards. Some even organize

Rule of Fit

crowd-pulling and interesting local tournaments on these lesser or non-standardized pitches. Whether you play in big world tournaments or championships or in local games, football games have the same rules.

The rule of fit in business states that any business is a subset of the entire world market; hence, it fits into it perfectly. No matter what you do, your business is only a dot in a big, circular world market. You can take any point within the market and fit in perfectly.

Just as spectators can enjoy a football game played by two teams each with eleven players or two teams each with five players; you can do successful business with as little capital as you can ever imagine. Some people have stifled their brilliant business ideas just because they have been waiting endlessly for the right time to get the needed capital to start their business. Unfortunately, such time may never come until you identify your niche and target them with little or no capital. Even in your market niche, you can still identify a smaller niche just in case your target niche seems too big in terms of capital requirement. For example, the whole market could be shoes. However, do you have the capacity to produce shoes for everyone? If your answer is 'No,' then you can think of targeting children by producing children shoes. However, it might also be difficult, based on your limited capital, for you to produce all shoe types for children. It now calls for you to consider whether to produce what shoe type for what age bracket.

The rule of fit teaches that every entrepreneur should know his limit (technical know-how/strength, capital strength, etc), understand his market niche and operate within the confines of his niche to succeed. If you understand the rule of fit in business, you will not owe your staff their salaries even in bad business weather. This is because, you would have understood that when a standard business within your industry which leverages on economy of scale, pays ₦y per capita to its workers, it would be unprofitable for your small business to pay the same ₦y per capita to your staff.

Do you know you can succeed in any venture you go into by simply understanding where you fit in? You do not have any business competing with big established businesses when you can simply create a niche for yourself and become a market leader and standard for others within your niche.

A few months to my wedding in 2013, I felt I needed a generator that could power all my electrical appliances most especially, my deep freezer and Electric iron. A 2.5KVA, 100% Copper Wire, Big Coil generator came to mind. Just when I was thinking of where I could buy a good one, I ran into my old school friend who lived not too far from me, in fact, he was living within the same local government area where I also lived. A few days after we ran into each other, I visited him at his rented apartment. He was living in the upper left 3-bedroom flat in a four-flat building. I noticed there was a big generator sitting at the corner of his balcony the moment we entered his apartment. As we got closer, it was a fairly used 2.5KVA gasoline generator.

Then I asked him a few details about the generator. He told me he had been using the generator since the past fifteen months. He told me the generator was very reliable. He said he only needed to do the servicing periodically and that was all. He then gave me the description of the place where he bought it. A week later, I went there to see if I could pick up the exact generator I saw at my friend's place. It was a local market where various household items are sold. As I entered the very street my friend described, I noticed that every store on that street was selling generating sets of different types and brands.

As I moved further down the street, a shop owner who suspected I needed some help walked to me and advertised four different brands of generator and also explained their capacities within one minute. As if that was not enough, he even promised to make transportation arrangement to ease the movement of the generator to wherever I was going. This got me I must confess to you. When he was done speaking, I asked him to take me to his shop. At his shop, I saw the very type of generator my friend was using and then I asked him if the brand was the best among them all. He then showed me another generator with better quality, strength, durability, fuel efficiency and higher specification. Although it came with a higher price, I had no doubt about his sense of judgment because of his charming first impression.

On that street alone, I could estimate the number of generator sellers to be around thirty. But out of thirty, only one succeeded in selling a generator to me. Does it mean others would not make it in that market? No, it doesn't. It was the after sales service the man advertised to me that really got me. Others too might have their respective Unique Selling Propositions (USPs). Perhaps, it could be competitive pricing, better shop display, convenient or user-friendly shopping, better payment options (like POS terminal or even installmental payment options), after sales service (repairs and maintenance), free coffee drink, beverages, snacks, and so on.

If you can identify a particular unique selling proposition that works for your business, even if everyone on your street sells the same item as you do, your business will still be profitable.

Rule of Fit 16

CHAPTER THREE
RULE OF REPLACEMENT

© FIFA.com

In the game of football, eleven players are permitted to play in an official match while the maximum number of substitutes permissible in a game is between three and five, depending on the type of competition.

A business is a business and football is a game. However, in some way, a business is a football game and a football game is a business. In a football game, the overall winner lifts a trophy and gets some financial rewards. An entrepreneur, though, does not lift a trophy after weathering a boisterous business storm; he gets a reward for his hard work, that is, profit. By this we can comfortably say that a business is a football game. Seeing how global businesses Like CocaCola, Adidas, Wanda, Hyundai, Qatar Airways and Visa partner with FIFA, it is not out of place to say that the football game is a business.

If there is provision for substitution up to a maximum of between three and five in an official game, I believe every business owner or would-be entrepreneurs should adopt substitution strategy in their business.

Why is substitution necessary in a game of football?
Not all eleven players can play a full match of ninety minutes without being fatigued, hence, the need for substitution. Some players, in the course of a game, could get injured and might need to be substituted. Also, for tactical reasons, for example, bringing on a striker in place of a defender; substitution may be necessary. And finally, if a player's performance gets lower than expected; such a player may be substituted.

Just as there is substitution bench in a game of football, there should be reserve capital in startups or existing businesses. Although many big businesses do operate reserve capital policies, it is very uncommon to find small businesses that operate reserve capital policy. There exist different nomenclatures for reserve capital in big businesses. Some companies call it retained profits, retained earnings, buffer capital, bank capital, and so on. Like substitution bench in a football game, reserve capital in any business is used to cater for contingencies or to offset capital losses.

It is a fact that ninety percent (90%) of new startups fail, 75% of venture-backed startups fail, under 50% of businesses make it to their fifth year, only 40% of startups actually turn a profit and 82% of businesses that fail do so because of cash/capital problems. Going by the last statistics above, it is not out of place to say that, most businesses or startups that fail do so because of poor capital management.

If three players (which represent 21.4% of the registered team) are reserved on the bench to buffer eleven players playing on the field, why wouldn't an entrepreneur reserve some buffer capital for the purpose of offsetting capital losses? As players sustain injuries or get fatigued in the course of a game, so do businesses run into bad business weather or run into unfriendly or unfavourable external environmental factors. These factors deplete or eat up the invested capital and the only thing to do is buffer the depleted capital with the reserve capital or, in the case of an existing business, plough back the retained earnings into the business.

If you have a business that is less than five years and you are already thinking of folding it up because it is not producing profit, then your business is probably among the over 50% businesses that do not make it to their fifth year. It will not be out of place for you to look for people who are doing something similar to yours and have stayed in it successfully for over five years. Get them to mentor you to success.

During my second year as a writer, I felt something was not just right about the way I was going about my profession. I decided to submit myself for training under an experienced, prolific and renowned writer and playwright to learn the technicalities of the writing profession. After the training, my approach and thinking about writing changed and since then, I have been enjoying tremendous and steady growth.

If you are a small business proprietor you would understand what it means to run a small business. As a sole proprietor, the challenges of separating personal money from the money meant for the business is so huge that only an insignificant number of entrepreneurs can overcome this daunting temptation. A school proprietor once told me that she used the school fees of about **One Hundred and Three Thousand Naira (N103,000.00)** that was paid into her account to repair her private car and to buy some personal effects for herself.

She was able to do this because she was not operating a separate bank account for her school. It was her personal bank account that she was using for the school. Many people reading this piece right now that are business owners are like this woman. You domicile business money in your personal account while you are holding your personal account's debit card in your hands. How can you ever resist the temptation of spending your business funds for your personal needs?

After officially registering my business, the next thing I did was to open a separate account for my business. I deliberately refused to use a debit card for the account. In fact, I was given the option of a cheque but I vehemently refused to use a cheque. Do not get me wrong, I am not saying anything was wrong with using a cheque book for your business. It was just that I personally chose not to use it. Holding a cheque book in my hand was just like holding a debit card. I preferred to use the internet banking platform because it offered me the leisure of making easy transfers to the bank accounts of my staff.

If you are thinking of starting a new business, please take note of the following:

Set aside additional 20% fund outside your 100% business capital. For example, if your total capital requirement is $1,000, set aside at least another $200 in a separate account. The $200 should be kept for unforeseen business contingencies or capital losses. Naturally, these things will come in the course of business. Many businesses did not foresee COVID-19 coming at the time it came but it did come. Only a few businesses that operated the reserve capital were able to sail through this challengingly stormy period.

If you are yet to operate the reserve capital policy in your business, please begin now and if you once operated it but stopped at some point, restart and sustain it. It is a life saver.

Rule of Replacement 22

CHAPTER FOUR

RULE OF FAIR PLAY

© MasterFile

According to **International Fair Play Committee**, fair play is a complex concept that comprises and embodies a number of fundamental values that are not only integral to sport but relevant in everyday life. It refers to *fair competition, respect, friendship, team spirit, equality, excellence, sportsmanship, sport without doping, respect for rules, solidarity, tolerance and care.*

Rule of Fair Play

The emboldened or italicized concepts in the above paragraph, according to International Fair Play Committee, are also known as fundamental values of fair play. They must be applied in all sporting activities in order to enjoy the fruits of success. Talking about enjoying the fruits of success, it is not just enough to win, **Triumph** must be measured by absolute fair means, honesty and just play.

Simon Chepat was a long-distance Kenyan runner and strong contender in the Okpekpe International 10-kilometer Road Race. Okpekpe International Road Race is an annual road race that usually holds sometime in May in Edo State, Nigeria. During the 2019 edition of the race, Simon Chepat, who came first in the 2016 edition of the competition, displayed a high sense of sportsmanship by helping his rival and fellow Kenyan runner, Kenneth Kipkemoi, who collapsed near the finish line, to get to the finish line. Although Simon came fifteenth in this edition of the competition, his magnanimity and act of kindness attracted so much attention from a number of spectators. He later earned kind donations of not less than $10,000 as a result of this noble gesture.

Even though Simon did not lift the trophy, he stole the show and also won the hearts of many who are on the same page with International Fair Play Committee as regards the belief that, in sport, winning trophies alone is not enough, but winning them by applying fundamental values of fair play as ingredients is what brings success.

In today's market place or market space, it will be impossible for any marketer of products or services to succeed if he does not imbibe the fundamental values of fair play. Precisely, it will be difficult for a marketer in today's world to succeed without maintaining an effective relationship with his customers. This is because there are too many products or services out there in the market and unfortunately, buyers are wary of making the wrong purchase decision. Everyone feels good and satisfied when he makes a good purchase or when he perceives the purchase he just made is worth his money. On the other hand, for every bad purchase, a buyer feels uncomfortable. This makes them to be suspicious of the marketer in their subsequent purchases.

This suspicion makes it a hard work for any marketer to easily sell his product or service in the market. Only marketers that have what it takes to maintain an effective relationship with customers will have a greater advantage over competition.

This suspicion is higher in intangible products (like services) than in tangible products. Thus, if you are a marketer of intangible products, be willing to do more of relationship selling/marketing. This will go a long way in making your penetration seamless.

There was a particular organization that I approached in July 2019 for the purpose of introducing to them my first book, Practical Emotional Intelligence In The Workplace. Having tried all my marketing skills, I gave up on the chase. Then sometime in 2020, out of genuine care for the growth of the organization, I offered free business advice and even went a step further by giving free copy of the book to the proprietor of this organization. Surprisingly, the same man who rejected my book, ordered many copies for his members of staff.

What made the difference was neither the copy of my book that I gave out for free nor my free advice. It was my genuine care for the growth of the organization occasioned by my readiness to maintain and sustain an effective relationship with the proprietor.

Before a relationship between you and your prospect or customer is engaged, there had existed a heightened level of suspicion on his part. Your task, therefore, is to find a way to reduce this suspicion by showing your interest is not purely on his money, but on solving identified problems for him. If you can succeed in earning his trust, the relationship you have successfully maintained and sustained will sell the product/service without you lifting a finger.

Relationship selling is a great strategy that should form an integral part of an integrated marketing strategy in any organization, especially, service-based ones. Where other strategies fail, relationship selling will succeed.

Successful businesspeople know the Chinese word **guanxi**, its Japanese version **ningen kankei** and its Latin American version **compadre** which all refer to friendship, human relations or attaining a level of trust. These people are very much aware that there is no substitute for establishing friendship in some cultures before effective business negotiations can take place. For example, a prospective Arab business associate will offer coffee as part of the important ritual of establishing a level of friendship and trust; and you should accept, even if you only take a ceremonial sip.

Another fundamental value of fair play is team spirit. Every football coach understands the importance team spirit. They understand that it is possible to take highly skillful individual players to a pitch of play and lose against a highly disciplined team of unskilled or amateur players.

What made Nigeria to triumph over Brazil at the semi-finals of the 1996 Olympic football tournament was team spirit. Judging by individual skills of the Brazilian team, they stood a better chance than Nigeria. Of course, this was proven in the score line up till the 77th minute. From the 78th minute, the more disciplined side, being Nigeria, showed that there was more to winning than just possessing individual skill. They proved that winning has so much to do with discipline and team spirit as they leveled up the score line to 3-3. They went further to score the deciding goal within the first three minutes of extra time.

As it is in football, so it is in business. A business that must succeed in today's market place or market space must encourage team spirit among its team members. Every member must focus on the goal of the business and must also work in an integrated and coordinated manner to achieve this goal. Any deviation from this is disastrous to the health of the organization.

As the team is working towards achieving the organization's goal, they must do it with every sense of solidarity, tolerance and care. It is not impossible that, in achieving this goal, one or more members may sustain injury, casualty, fatality, pain, sickness and discouragement. It will be wrong to abandon these individuals or assume that the goal could still be achieved without them. No coach abandons his injured player on the field of play and focus on others who are fit. They take care of them and substitute them with players that are fit in the event that they can no longer continue the match.

Sport without doping is another fundamental value of fair play. This value is as important as other values of fair play and it is one element that can mar business success if not well managed. A lot of business organizations involve in sharp practices both internally and externally without considering the fact that there is a price to pay in the long run. One may cheat to have one's way in the short run, but, in the long run, everyone in the team pays dearly for it.

The debilitating effect of cheating is same whether in the business circle, political sphere, religious circle or any other sectors. Cheating relegates meritocracy and elevates mediocrity. For example, a company that supports and permits tribalism and nepotism in its employment process cannot operate excellently as it has already compromised the very foundation of fair play.

Respect for rules is also an essential value of fair play. If everyone in the organization can have respect for established code of conduct in the business place, the business will succeed and so will the staff members. A rule as simple as lateness to work can negatively impact the business growth if not well handled. Everyone in the organization should have respect for this rule as failure to do so by a member or failure by management to take a stand on the rule can make other members of the organization see lateness as normal code of practice.

CHAPTER FIVE

RULE OF REWARD

© **Premier Skills English**

There is no gainsaying the fact that footballers are among the highest paid people in the world. They enjoy fabulous financial rewards/compensations for their performances.

In the English Professional football players are commonly remunerated by their clubs by way of a basic wage (usually expressed as £x thousand per week) and additionally with bonus payments based on the achievement of a variety of different targets.

Clubs will usually provide a fixed bonus amount for every match in which a player appears. This is called appearance fees. However, the nature of such bonuses varies from player to player depending on their years of experience in professional footballing, rating and play time.

There is also loyalty bonus which is paid to players at a specified future date, provided that the player is still employed by the club at that time. Other bonuses include goal bonuses for forward players or goal-scoring midfielders, defenders and goalkeepers.

All the fees and bonuses above are huge if compared to the salaries of an average worker anywhere in the world. This is why almost all footballers are on pressure to deliver high performances to their clubs or countries whenever in the field of play. Most of the time, you get to see them display emotions whenever they win or lose a game.

You wonder why a fully grown thirty-four year old married man who, perhaps, has two kids back home could be sobbing uncontrollably in front of tens of thousands watchful spectators and millions of audience on TV. It is partly for the love of the game as well as for the money. It is not just a trophy that has been lost, or a CV that has been dented; it is also about some financial rewards that have been forfeited.

In the build-up to the 2014 World Cup, the Nigerian Football Federation had promised its international squad, the Super Eagles, that it would advance the team a match bonus of $10,000 for a win and a $5,000 for every match drawn. These incentives encouraged the team to go all out against Kenya during the World Cup qualifier to beat them 1-0.

As a result of financial difficulties which led to pay cuts to back room staff working with its various international teams, the federation reduced the bonuses $10,000 for a win and $5,000 for a draw to $5,000 and $2,500 respectively. This made the team to refuse to travel to the Confederations Cup in Brazil. The sports ministry had to intervene in the matter by making extra money available for the team to travel to Brazil.

It goes therefore to prove that financial rewards play an important role in motivating staff to work for the success of the organization. I have personally noticed that the time an employee is most active is the first week. This is because it is the pay week. By the second week when he must have shared his salary according to plan, he starts to get fatigued. He is feeling this way because his salary is almost depleted. By the time he gets to the third week, he is completely down both mentally and physically. By the fourth week, his morale increases because salary is approaching.

If organizations could design a compensation plan that incorporates weekly pay-out/bonuses to their staff members, motivation will increase and performance will also be heightened. Apart from the fact that good compensation plan for staff members improves their performance, it keeps their minds focused on the goal and takes their minds off any sharp practices. How do you expect that your Customer Relations Officer who has a daily job task of receiving cash from customers will not be tempted to convert such money for personal use when his monthly pay cannot even take care of an average worker's living expense?

Some employers do think that the only way to reduce labour turnover is by increasing workloads or by increasing hours of work. They erroneously think that labour turnover or low performance is due to leisure time allowed by the organization. Hence they further tighten the system either by increasing workloads, or by increasing hours of work or by even laying off some staff members in order to put work pressure on the existing staff. By this, they believe, the existing staff will have little or no time left to pursue their dreams of a better job or a new business.

This is not only unfair, it is counter-productive. If you want your staff's loyalty to your business to improve, pay them well. It is not just enough to pay them handsomely, consider a compensation plan that is workable, attractive and effective. Like I mentioned earlier, the third week of the month is usually fraught with fatigue, hence, an employer can advance stipends to his employees as a way of motivating them for higher performance.

Rewards should not only be limited to monthly pay or bonus payment. Employers should find a way of appreciating excellent or outstanding performance. There are employees in your organization that are working round the clock, not to impress you, but genuinely to ensure that the business does not fail. They consciously follow up on past performances of the business in order improve performance and then surpass historical records. They set new peak and work towards achieving it.

While others are busy taking annual leaves not because they really need it for a particular purpose, these high flyers stay back to ensure the business does not suffer any setback. They are there for the company through thick and thin. To the lazy ones, these individuals are a major threat as they often make them look like they are not doing anything at all.

If you have such people in your organization, do not hesitate to treat them well. They are your number one asset after your customers. Ensure that you reward them for their excellent or outstanding performance.

At the end of a major football competition, outstanding performers are rewarded. To some, it is the Man of the match and to some; it is the Most Valuable Player (MVP). All these awards and rewards are just a way of motivating performance. This rewards system can be replicated and applied to business to improve performance.

Financial rewards, as a means of motivating performance, are very good. However, it is very important to also talk about non-financial rewards.

During a football match, the scoreboard is conspicuously displayed for the players to see their current performance. Apart from the scoreboard, time is also displayed to tell them to increase performance as time is fast ticking.

Instead of a scoreboard, a marketing organization could use a leaderboard for posting sales representatives' performance. Although, this system may produce unhealthy rivalry among the sales reps, it can be used positively by the team lead to improve performance. Sales reps who are lagging behind will be motivated to improve.

Acknowledging team members' achievements for a job well done is also very important. However this method must be properly done. When using this method, there is no small achievement. In other words, every small achievement is worth appreciating. Mention names and praise them genuinely for their performances. Let them know that their contribution is appreciated.

For milestone achievement, make public recognition in order to encourage others. Printed letters will particularly be effective in this regard. Let your outstanding performers feel important about what they have helped the organization to achieve.

It is also possible that there are sales reps who are not in the category of high flyers. For some of them who have performed above their personal period best, they need some encouragements. To encourage them, acknowledge their little contributions to the overall achievement of the business. This encourages everyone, from high flyers to everyone else, to keep on improving.

Let's be reminded that, in football, the trophy is not given to an individual but to the team. Therefore, performing teams in a business should be rewarded for their performance. Trophies should be rotated from one team to another monthly and the winning team should be celebrated for their outstanding performance. Hence, healthy competition should not only be limited to individuals, it should be extended to teams. By this, the organization's overall performance will improve.

CHAPTER SIX

RULE OF TIMING

© ScoreVision

Every standard football match is played within ninety (90) minutes with a change of ends and an interval of not more than fifteen (15) minutes. There are two halves of forty-five (45) minutes each. In the case of a draw, and, depending on the rules of the competition, a result may be reached by an extra time of thirty (30) minutes duration or a penalty shoot-out.

Why ninety (90) minutes for a match duration?

Let's educate ourselves on how the length of a football match came about. We may have to cast our minds back in time to the north of England when the game was just beginning. In many parts of the country, the various football associations were responsible for creating their own rules, with no standard set of rules having yet been formed.

The Sheffield rules were one of the chief rules used then. It later spread from Yorkshire to the north of England and to the midlands. In 1866, London and Sheffield went up against each other in a match and had to decide how long it should last for, with both associations having matches of different lengths at that time. Even the concept of changing ends at half time had only been introduced to the Sheffield Rules in 1862, but even that was dependent on there having been no goals scored in the first period of play. It is believed that the two teams agreed on a match of ninety (90) minutes, with people feeling that the length was suitable as the players would be tired by the end of it.

There is likelihood that the London clubs tended to play the Football Association rules, which set the time of a match at a shorter duration to the 2 hours that the Sheffield Association thought play should take place for. Compromise was reached and set at 45 minutes per half for a total of 90 minutes, even though, this was not made official until 1897. **(History adapted from Football Stadiums at https://www.football-stadiums.co.uk/articles/football-timings-and-match-lengths/)**

From the above historical background, it is obvious that there were conflicts of interests as to whether a shorter match duration should be chosen instead of a longer match duration or vice versa. The proponents of both schools of thought had valid points to prove. For example, shorter duration would make the game uninteresting as no goals might be scored by either teams while longer duration could bring about boredom on the part of the spectators and fatigue on the part of the players.

In the end, a near realistic and achievable match duration was set at 90 minutes, which, since 1897, has never been altered till date. There is a whole lot of cue to take from soccer match duration. If it can work for soccer it can work for business, politics, religious organizations or any other life's endeavour. Many entrepreneurs set targets for themselves or for their teams which are either too low or too high. Many a time, these targets are given inappropriate timings – they are either too long or too short and sometimes, some of these targets are not even given any timings at all. They just approach issues haphazardly without any concrete plans as to how to achieve their goal.

If you must be successful in whatever you do, set time duration for carrying out or completing a task. For example, if you are nursing a dream of starting a business that has an initial capital requirement of ₦1Million, you must state exactly when you would start it. Let's say you are currently under paid employment with a monthly salary of ₦100,000, and out of your salary, it is possible for you to conveniently save ₦50,000 in a month. It is therefore commonsensical to put the timing of starting your dream business at one year and eight months, all things being equal or at two years, taking into consideration time value of money.

Rule of Timing

It will be unrealistic to set the timing at six months as your personal savings will only be ₦300,000, just 30% of the required capital. Also, it will be uneconomical to set the timing at three (3) years. Marty Allen once said that a study of Economics usually reveals that the best time to buy anything is last year. In other words, do what you should do today today and not at a future date as you may have to spend more to do it tomorrow, only if the opportunity will still be available then.

Case for consideration

As a team lead working in a power company, you have just had deliberation with your team of CROs (Customer Relations Officers)/marketers on a Monday morning. Part of the discussions was to change the narratives about your cash collection drive in the new week. Your strategy was to embark on a street-to-street publicity within your sales territory in a bid to encourage your consumers to pay their outstanding debts. Having resolved to use two days in the week for the exercise, you moved to other equally important matters affecting sales and growth of your service unit. Soon, the meeting ended and every member of your team was in high spirit.

In the course of the week, there arose unprecedented challenges like the official vehicle which developed a mechanical fault on Tuesday. By Thursday, it was fixed and was in perfect shape. Other minor challenges also came up but they were all resolved in the week. You and the rest of the team were overwhelmed by the challenges so much so that you did not realize that you had not done the planned publicity until it was Friday.

From the above case, there is obviously something that you could have done differently which you failed to do. You ought to have chosen the two days (Say, Monday and Wednesday) for the publicity and possibly, you could have also chosen the time and responsibilities. By responsibilities I mean, you should have selected and assigned CROs who would go out for the exercise. It is often said that everybody's responsibility is nobody's responsibility. Since you have failed to assign people to carry out the task, you should not expect that the task would be carried out.

Challenges are normal occurrences in life. So, you would still have found a way of surmounting the challenges and still move on with the plan. Most of the time when people do not get things done, it is not that they cannot really get those things done, it is that they have no commitment to getting them done. Discussing a plan alone is not enough to getting a plan carried out. What you need to effectively carry out a plan are:
- Writing down the plan;
- Setting a time frame for carrying it out;
- Assigning people to carry out the plan;
- Supervising them to ensure that the plan is well carried out

One of many challenges that marketing managers grapple with is setting targets for their teams. There is really no hard and fast rule about setting target other than by available information gathered from marketing activities and from company's strategic objectives. Prior to the universal acceptance of ninety (90) minutes as match duration, the different football associations in England had tested both the high duration of two hours and the low duration of less than two hours before finally agreeing at a realistic duration of ninety (90) minutes.

Many marketing managers are not setting realistic targets. This is because their targets are not a product of scientific evaluation but that of guesswork. The resultant effect of their instinctive targets is exhaustion, fatigue and frustration on the part of the sales team. The targets are often set too high than they can ordinarily meet Depending on your industry, you can set **SMART (Specific, Measurable, Attainable, Relevant and Tine-bound)** targets that are optimal enough for business growth by applying the following steps:

➢ Analyze company/management's expectation – What is the company seeking to achieve?
➢ Review company's strategic objectives – What are the company's medium to long term goals?
➢ Prioritize the selected objectives
➢ Quantify the objectives
➢ Collect data from marketing activities
➢ Analyze the data collected and make forecast
➢ Set the targets
➢ Set action plan – organize responsibility and set time frame for every target set;
➢ Review the plan with all stakeholders and covet their consensus
➢ Implement plan and constantly review results in line with current realities.

CHAPTER SEVEN

RULE OF RECESS

© E&E News

Soccer is one game that has undergone (and still is undergoing) series of tests and has been trusted by billions of people around the world as a game for all. About a half of the world's population form the fan base of this great sport. No sport in the world has intimidating fan base like soccer. Soccer is not just a game; it is a formidable authority in the world of sport.

Having said this, it is important to know that soccer did not just get to this stage by happenstance; it has, like gold, passed through fire. History records that the earliest known form of soccer was played in China during the Han Dynasty, in a game called 'Cuju', translated literally as 'Kick Ball'. However, modern day soccer was founded in England in the 1880s with the formation of the Football Association (FA) which standardized the rules for competition.

Talking about tests or modifications, soccer has been modified a number of times and now, it is near perfection. No wonder it is the world's most favorite sport. Part of its modification is the recess/break time. In the ninety (90) minutes soccer game, there is a fifteen (15) minutes recess. This is permitted at the end of the first half of 45 minutes. This time is allowed to make the players cool off and to prevent exhaustion or fatigue.

Research has found that taking a break can be very beneficial for you and your work/business. Short breaks, lunch-time breaks and longer breaks have all been shown to have a positive relationship with well-being and productivity. By taking regular breaks you can boost your performance. Studies have also found that breaks can reduce/prevent stress, help to maintain performance throughout the day and reduce the need for a long recovery at the end of the day.

Stress, exhaustion or fatigue can affect one's body, thoughts, feelings, and behaviour. Originators of soccer and its handlers alike, have a good understanding of this position, hence, their modification of the game to accommodate breaks in-between a soccer match.

To every entrepreneur or business owner, productivity is key. And, profitability is a function of productivity. When productivity reduces, profitability is adversely affected. However, not every entrepreneur understands that, to prevent low performance, it is important to allow teams to take a break at intervals within a day at work and within a year.

A couple of years ago, I had an excruciating pain around my upper back down to my waist and even more at my waist. It was so severe that I almost thought I had a disjointed spine or what some medical professionals call the slipped disc.. It was always a difficult thing for me to stand upright. Bending at 90% was completely impossible. In fact, I dare not do jumps because it was as if my vertebra column would snap.

I used all prescribed medications but the pain would not subside. I then thought of what I had been doing a few months before the pain started. It was not as if I involved myself in any form of extreme sports and neither did I lift any heavy objects. I did not even involve myself in any hard labour. The only thing I remembered I did was sitting for up to 10 hours at a stretch in most of the days of the week and of the month writing. It was a period in my writing career that I needed to increase productivity. It was also a time to build for me and for my career. So, I had to spend more time sitting at the same spot for hours. Worthy of mention, also, is the fact that, during this period of pain, I could hardly concentrate while writing. My mental capacity dropped a bit lower than when I was without pain.

Having realized that the pain I was feeling was due to my long hours of sitting, I stopped writing for about two weeks. Within the first three days of my break from writing, I felt a bit relieved even without taking any pills. By the time it was exactly one week, I was almost feeling I should resume writing. At exactly two weeks, the pain was completely gone.

Managers or entrepreneurs who want to see improved performance in their businesses must be more employee-oriented than task/target-oriented.. It is important to meet targets or to complete tasks. However, what gain does it bring meeting targets or completing tasks with necks broken? Of what use is your met targets when almost all your team members have lost morale as a result of fatigue, sickness, injury, or, in a worst case scenario, death?

Think of a football team that has six matches in a month to play in order to win a championship. Assuming in its first successful match, 50% of its players sustain major injuries that will take up to a month to heal. It means the team would be missing in action its best legs in its second match. Assuming again, the coach pushes the team too hard so much so that they have to win the second match with 50% of its player down with major injuries that will last for a month. The team may this time, now have to rely on its backup players to win the remaining matches. The chances of the team winning its subsequent matches may, at this point, be subject to imagination.

A good manager should be more interested in his team's welfare especially, as regards breaks both intra-work and long breaks. If you notice stress, or fatigue in your employee, recommend he must take a break, and, if his annual leave is still unused, recommend he takes a long break from work to allow for proper rest. Do not be a manager that wears a frown each time his team member approaches him for casual leave or annual leave. Taking these breaks is good both for the employee and the business. Also, do know that it costs five times more to get a new employee than maintaining an existing one, says, Philip Kotler. So, maintain your staff and treat them well so they can in turn pay you back with improved performance or better output.

CHAPTER EIGHT

RULE OF TRAINING

© WikiMedia Commons

One sport that encourages training among players is soccer. Before a major competition is played, professional footballers do train together in training camps to position themselves for a win. No team goes into a football competition for the sake of exchanging pleasantries with other teams. Their objective is to win the trophy. Training is necessary for bonding among the players and for

Rule of Training

sharpening their skills. Usually, individual players are talented in their own right, but, if they do not train together something important will be missing in the team – that is, team spirit. It is team spirit that makes the team play in a unique way that only the players in the team can understand. Outsiders cannot understand the team as much as members can. For example, as a member of a football team, if you do understand your team very well, it will be much easier to know what each of them can do with the ball in the 18-yard box. Say, you are left with no option other than make an emergency pass to Player A who is surrounded by four desperate defenders in the 18-yard box, and you know too well that Player A is very good at scissors kick even when the situation is tight. Your instinct should tell you, having bonded very well with Player A, that you should make a chip ball pass so that he can conveniently do his scissors kick.

Teams that win competitions are those with high team spirit. They are teams that have bonded very well as a result of having understood one another. A bonded team helps one another to sharpen their skills and strengths and to support the weaknesses of one another. They play with high level of discipline and character in an integrated manner. Player A does not say, "I am a striker, it is Player C's responsibility, as a left fullback player, to defend the goal post during corner kicks..

Many entrepreneurs use the term, team spirit without fully understanding its real meaning. The real and true meaning of team spirit in business is compared to a customer who approaches an Admin personnel of a marketing firm to make a simple enquiry about the firm's product that has, for two weeks, been in short supply. The customer says, **"Hello Madam, May I, please, know** *why your XYZ (product) has been in short supply since two weeks ago?"* Before the customer lands, the Admin personnel interrupts and says, *"Sorry Ma, I am not a marketer, you can contact the marketing people in the open office over there to make your enquiries."* This shows that there is no team spirit in the firm. The firm's production/marketing weakness should not have been exposed, but defended and supported by every other member of the team. If every member of the team had been trained to know a bit of everything in other units of the firm, the situation that ensued between the customer and the Admin personnel would not have occurred.

Entrepreneurs or team leads should create an atmosphere that allows teams within their organizations to bond by disseminating information and conducting training regularly. Every member of the team should have, first-hand, information concerning the business, its products or customers before the customers. It will be highly embarrassing and absurd that a customer has to inform a company's staff about his company's product, advert placement or any other information concerning the company. Many businesses make regular updates on their websites or other social media channels without first informing their own staff about these updates. Sometimes, these staff only get to know about these information through an outsider. This is highly embarrassing.

If it is possible for a soccer team with great individual talents to lose against a less talented but well bonded team; it is also very possible for an organization with highly qualified/skilled employees to perform poorly because the team lacks positive attitude, discipline and the right training. Individuals in such a team are more focused on their skills, qualification, status and achievements and less focused on the corporate objectives of the business. They operate in atmosphere of unhealthy rivalry/competition, which does not promote growth and progress.

Many organizations, especially the small (and sometimes the medium sized) ones, do not conduct formal trainings to their newly employed members of staff. Most often, they do crash programmes which are not very effective. It is even worse with medium sized organizations because they outsource part of their HR functions to syndicate or third party organizations who do not fully grasp the intricacies of the business. They hand out peripheral training and leave out the real bone and core part of the business. Unfortunately, these syndicate third party organizations are handicapped financially and are unable to carry out thorough training exercises on behalf of their principals. As a result of this financial constraint, they cannot conduct the kind of training that can position the new employees suitably for their new roles.

Small organizations on the other hand, do not have the financial backbone to conduct any formal training; hence, they rely on the existing staff to put the new employees through in their new roles. This may be economical but it definitely comes with debilitating effect to the overall objective of the business.

Apart from the training conducted for the newly employed, the following trainings are also needed for better bonding and productivity:

I. Technical Training – This is a type of training meant to teach the new employees the technical aspect of the job. For example, a training on how to use the computer system (CRM) to find new prospects;

II. Quality Training – This is important in a production-oriented company where employees must familiarize themselves with means of preventing, detecting and eliminating non-quality items in order to produce safe products;

III. Skills Training – This is all about proficiencies required for actual performance of the job. For example, marketer that is being trained on how to cold-call;

IV. Soft Skills Training – This refers to training on other things that help one to perform one's core function seamlessly. For example, training on how to be friendly and warm to customers;

V. Professional Training – This refers to training conducted for professionals and it is usually done by professional bodies of respective professions. For example, periodic seminars conducted by the National Institute of Marketing of Nigeria (NIMN) for professional marketers;

VI. Team Training – This type of training is highly important for team building. It facilitates relationship building and empowers team to improve decision making, problem solving and team development skills to achieve business results. The goal of this training is to develop cohesiveness among team members, allowing them to get to know one another for the purpose of working for a common objective.

CHAPTER NINE
RULE OF DIFFERENTIATION

© **Liverpool FC**

Two teams in a soccer match must necessarily wear jersey colours that distinguish them from each other. Premier League rules state, "When playing in league matches the player of each participating club shall wear strip which is of a sufficient contrast that match officials, spectators and television viewers will be able to distinguish clearly between the two teams."

Colours play a vital role in soccer and indeed, among different teams both on the pitch and off the pitch. Colours have two major benefits and they are; to identify a team and to distinguish them. Whenever you see a national team wearing a jersey with green and white colours, then it is not unlikely the team is from Nigeria. Similarly, during the English Premier League match, the team that will most likely use a red jersey would be Liverpool FC.

To the two teams mentioned above, their respective colours are a mark of identification and distinction. It will be highly absurd and confusing, for example, if the Nigerian national team is seen wearing a yellow jersey or the Liverpool team wearing a pink jersey.

Apart from the fact that colours distinguish or identify teams, different teams have strong emotional attachments to their chosen colours as they believe their wins or triumphs are dependent on them. A Liverpool team will most likely win a match if they wear a red jersey than if they wear a pink one.

As colours have a powerful effect on team's emotions in soccer, so do they in business and other life's endeavour. In business, colours have powerful effects on our emotions and these emotions play a major role in how we behave as consumers. At times, you come across a certain colour and what crosses your mind is a particular product or company. This is no coincidence; the company has successfully impressed the colour on your psyche through promotional activities over time. In fact, if you had not been properly informed and educated, you would think the company created or owned the colour.

Successful entrepreneurs are those who understand the

importance of differentation. They know they must position their offerings right in the minds of their customers and their prospects. Philip Kotler said, and I paraphrase, "There are too many products that, in the eyes of the consumers, there is no difference." Sometimes you get to a local store to buy your favourite item, and after spending so much time looking for it; the sales attendant tells you it is out of stock but you could pick others on the shelf. He/she may even end up convincing you to buy close substitutes on the grounds that they offer same benefits. This confirms the earlier position by Philip Kotler above.

What has really happened in the above situation is that the original product you intended to purchase has a low brand equity. Philip Kotler defines brand equity as "the positive differential effect that knowing the brand name has on customer response to the product or service. Brand equity results in customers showing a preference for one product over another. When a product has a high brand equity, customers will respond with a high brand loyalty.

The above, though, does not come by happenstance. It is as a result of concerted and deliberate position and differentiation strategies adopted by success-focused entrepreneurs. You must differentiate your product from competition to earn market share as market share is not bought but earned.

Entrepreneurs must constantly think of what they can do to differentiate their products or services from competition. And they have to do so while considering the fact that time is irredeemable. Philip Kotler says, "Today, you have to run faster to stay in the same place." In other words, there are competing brands that are constantly fighting hard to become market leaders, and, if you sit back doing little or nothing to differentiate and position your brand favourably in the market place or market space, your brand could be swallowed up by better brands. If you keep doing what you are presently doing in your business for the next five years, without changing or flipping your approach and strategies, you may not be in business.

How Can I Differentiate My Product/Service?

Look inwards and consider the areas where your strength lies. If you are an entrepreneur whose personal core value is honesty, you would do well to promote a value statement of integrity in your business. People are quite comfortable dealing with organizations with high integrity. They can trust you with their money since they know it is in safe hands. People with high integrity are often successful in running financial institutions like commercial banks, micro-finance banks, payment service banks, and so on.

If you hate it if you have to spend long hours on queue accessing a service that you know too well that it should not take you more than a few minutes, then, it is unlikely you would compromise on speed when you start your business. Part of your personal core values would definitely be speed and this should form part of your value statements in business. You have to invest in technology in order to provide faster service to your customers/clients. It means therefore, that, when you would be promoting your product/service, you must do that on a platter of speed. Also, any attempt to compromise on speed or spending on technology should be totally avoided.

CHAPTER TEN

RULE OF PENALTY

© Sportskeeda

In the game of football, penalty (also called a spot kick) is usually awarded when an offence is committed, for example, if a player commits a direct free kick offence inside their penalty area. Also, penalty shootout is used to determine which team is victorious after a drawn match.

It is possible that, in a ninety-minute football game, either team plays a match without the referee awarding a penalty. This is because the teams are playing the game according to the rules.

However, in a situation where the referee awards a penalty kick against a team, the affected team must have flouted a rule.

During a football game, when you hear that long blast of the whistle from the referee, especially when there is a clear infringement from either team inside the penalty area; a penalty is imminent. However, the penalty does not signal the end of the game. The game continues after the penalty.

Having played the penalty and scored, it is possible for the team, against which the penalty was scored, to win the game if they do not sustain further infringements or if they play strictly according to the rules.
There are evidences that teams that were ever down by a penalty kick for committing a foul did bounce back before the final whistle. In fact, they did not only level up, they even won the game. Penalty kicks awarded against a team out of fouls committed should not mean that all hope of winning the game is lost. Most teams that understand this position are the ones that come out victorious in football games. This is because they observe the game's rules better and they play it according to the rules. They are more careful, integrated, focused and goal-oriented.

In business or entrepreneurship, there is room for penalty. It is not impossible to be in business without a time for penalty or spot kick. It is not impossible to be in business without flouting some business rules. At every point in time when an infringement is committed in business, whistle blowing that signals a penalty must be made.

What is penalty in business?

Penalties are used to moderate the activities of teams, departments or units and individuals in any business in order to make them conform to set standards, rules and norms. They are awarded to correct deviations or against any teams, individuals, departments or units that do not observe set rules of business.

The definition above must not be confused with penalties used for regulating businesses that have external relationships with regulatory bodies or with organizations outside the periphery of the business. For example, a business in Nigeria must observe tax laws as stipulated by the Federal Inland Revenue Service (FIRS). For example, a company that fails to file tax returns (CIT) at a stipulated period pays a penalty fee. Another regulatory body which moderates business practice in Nigeria includes the Corporate Affairs Commission (CAC). This body requires that every public company must file increase in share capital with the body, failure of which attracts a penalty fee. All the penalties mentioned above with external regulatory bodies are not within the context of this book. While the former regulates the internal operations of the business, the latter regulates the business operations in relations to bodies outside the confines of the business.

Talking about penalties in business, there are penalties that are cautionary and there are those that are terminal. In a game of football, if the referee blows the whistle after a player just committed a foul inside his team's penalty area and a penalty is awarded against his team, the game resumes after the penalty shot is made. Whether the penalty is converted to a goal or not, the team still has a chance of winning the game. I call this type of penalty cautionary. However, having played the game for ninety minutes and there is no clear winner, the referee may decide to break the tie with a penalty. I call this type of penalty terminal.

Entrepreneurs must understand how to use both cautionary penalties and terminal penalties to engender smooth internal operations of the business. There are instances where an individual within the organization may have to be penalized for flouting business rules and there are also instances where another individual may have to be given terminal penalty for behaving in a manner contrary to the vision, mission, goals or objectives of the organization.

Forms of cautionary penalties:
- **Queries** – To query is to put a question to someone in order to request information about something or to demand explanation for something that is in doubt.
- **Warning Letters** – A warning letter is served an employee that has committed an offence for which the organization expects a positive change
- **Letter of Temporary Suspension of Service** – This letter is given to an employee who is undergoing investigation for gross misconduct or other disciplinary matter. The decision to either reinstate or dismiss the employee depends on the outcome of the investigation.

Forms of terminal penalties:

- Letter of Termination of Appointment
- Letter of Advice To Withdraw

A company does not necessarily need to offer an employee a severance package/benefit when his employment is terminated; rather, it is discretionary. A worker who is laid off through no fault of his own may be eligible to receive severance benefits. For mild offences or for offences beyond the control of the employees, more companies are now using Letters of Advice to Withdraw as against using Letters of Termination of Appointment. Although the two letters have the same objectives, they obviously come with different tones.

Occasions where cautionary penalties may become imperative in business:
- An employee that works at cross purposes with the company's rules;
- An employee that fails to achieve goals set for his unit/department or for the organization;
- A company's marketing staff who fails to meet his target repeatedly;
- A hospital pharmacy assistant that dispenses wrong medications;
- A company staff that sleeps during working hours;
- A production company's supervisor that allocates production task to an untrained staff;
- A supervisor in a production company who fails to make necessary requisition for raw materials needed for production;
- A supervisor in a power company that fails to ensure that his men are fully kitted for a fault clearing work;

- A team lead in a hospital who fails to organize adequate staff for the daily task within his department;
- A team lead in a marketing department whose performance falls short of company's target despite having received adequate support in terms of human resources, financial resources, materials and physical resources (equipment, work tools, etc).

Occasions where terminal penalties may become imperative in business:
- An employee that comes late to work incessantly;
- A store keeper that pilfers or converts stock kept under his watch;
- A company team lead/manager who runs a parallel organization as his employer's and who uses company's resources (human, financial, physical and material) to run his personal business;
- A company's purchasing officer who forges receipts with an intent to short-change or defraud his company;
- A company's account officer who connives with suppliers to short-change or defraud his company;
- An internal audit officer of a hospital who connives with other personnel within the organization to certify false units of materials/stock as true and correct values with the intent of short-changing/defrauding his hospital of the value certified in excess.
- A security personnel of a hospital who connives with the morgue attendant by failing to take proper records of a body (corpse) brought into the morgue with an intent to pocket all fees paid in respect of the body's admission up to discharge;
- A Customer Relations Officer of a power company who issues counterfeit receipts for his customers' payments with intent to convert such payments for personal use.

CHAPTER ELEVEN

RULE OF WHISTLE BLOWING

© BreakingViews

Whistle blowing is an essential part of the football game. Without whistle blowing, a football game will be awkward, chaotic and disorderly. Referees blow the whistle most often, when there is a foul play or when an infringement is committed by a player.

In the field of play football players do express emotions like trading insults, abusive gesticulations, assault or even physical harm. These emotions can only be checked by a referee's whistle. Imagine a football match without a whistle; the result can only be one thing – commotion.

Consider the case below:

Player A, during a group stage match was brought down on account of Player B's front sliding tackle, a play which got unnoticed by the referee. Player A, having felt cheated for the unintentional tackle and for the referee's refusal to blow the whistle, thought he would pay back whenever he had the opportunity to do same to Player B. During the second half of the game, Player B had a one-to-one chance with the Player A's goal keeper within the 18-yard box only for Player A to suddenly appear from behind Player B with a sliding tackle that swept both the latter and the ball outside the touchline. The referee immediately made a long blast of the whistle signaling a serious foul committed by Player A.

Player A intentionally played the hard tackles against Player B as a revenge for Player B's initial sliding tackle made against him but he was caught by the referee. But for the whistle of the impartial referee, Player A would have robbed Player B's team of their well-deserved penalty kick, the only goal that qualified them for the quarter finals.

Every entrepreneur should operate his business like the football game, knowing when to blow the whistle. Entrepreneurs, especially the sole proprietors, most of the time, play against the rules. This is due to the fact that, unlike the game of football where the player is different from the referee, in sole proprietorship, the player is also the referee. Therefore it makes it a herculean task for the player to blow the whistle against himself. Hence, fouls are committed at will unchecked. Entrepreneurs in other forms of business, including partnership, private and public limited liabilities, where there is more than one shareholder, have a better sense of responsibility and are hence, more committed to fair play.

What Is Whistle Blowing in Business
So far, so much has been said about whistle blowing in football. At this point, we shall be talking about the term in the context of business. Whistle blowing in business is a term that is used to refer to a cautionary tool for engendering strict compliance and adherence to business rules and fair play. Entrepreneurs, like football players, are often caught in their own emotional web, a situation which makes them to take certain irrational decisions that are not only harmful, but dangerous to the survival of their businesses. To ensure that entrepreneurs play the business game according to the rule, a system must be in place to check them. This system is called Whistle Blowing.

Some whistle blowing indicators in business
There are certain indicators that call for whistle blowing in business. When the following indicators flash at you, then it is time that you must blow the whistle:
- ➤ When there is an attempt to convert business money for personal use or frivolities;
- ➤ When there is an attempt to give out your product or service to a family member for free;

Rule of Whistle Blowing

- When there is an attempt to convert the product of your business or that of your employer for personal use; with or without an intention of replacing it later or paying for it later;
- When, as an employee in a business, you begin to sign in at work later than the time officially allowed;
- When you use the official hours for personal business;
- When you use the asset, property, equipment, consumables or materials of your business or your employer's business for personal gains;
- When you use a personal bank account to receive business money or vice versa. You may be wondering why it is a foul play to use business bank account to receive personal money. You should not be tempted to do this because each time you make a withdrawal of your personal money from your business account, the business loses. Bank charges (Commission on transaction or COT) are deducted from the account;
- When there is an attempt to spend business money saved, set aside or reserved for a certain purpose for other purposes;

The above list is not exhaustible. You can add yours based on the size or form of your business. However, there are exceptions to the rule of whistle blowing in business. These exceptions are applied only at the discretion of the whistle blower. It is the whistle blower that knows what decision would be the best choice for his business at the time of taking the decision. In the referee's discretion in the case earlier stated above, he felt Player A's front sliding tackle was not so bad enough to attract whistle blowing but Player B's back sliding tackle was a serious infringement and deserved a blast of the whistle. Similar exceptions can also be applied in business by an entrepreneur. The whistle blower or an entrepreneur may decide to ignore certain business foul plays if he feels ignoring it will not hamper the smooth operation of the business. For example, you may ignore whistle blowing where a customer insists that he wants to make payment/transfer through a particular bank. Say your business bank account is domiciled with XYZ Bank and your personal savings account is domiciled with ABC Bank and your customer says he would prefer to make payment through ABC Bank. The decision to accept payment through ABC Bank or through your personal bank account will not significantly hamper the smooth running of your business. So, whistle blowing in this case is immaterial. Also, an entrepreneur may ignore whistle blowing if he feels the business could suffer monumental loss. For example, a beverage company (fictitious) has been struggling with dwindling sales of its orange flavor soft drink. One of the company's customers who is also a renowned social media influencer, had posted on social media platform that his close associate was recently diagnosed of food poisoning after a gulp of the soft drink. He also said that, having carried out forensic examination of the content of the bottle, it was discovered that a foreign body, believed to be the remains of cockroach, in the bottle could have been responsible for his friend's avoidable hospitalization. The video went viral and attracted several negative comments from internet users around the world. The company initially ignored the news saying it was one of those social media junks until demand for the product dwindled to an unimaginable low level since it was first introduced. At the company's strategic management meeting, it was resolved that certain strategic steps be taken to disabuse people's minds about the viral news. The steps included, among others, a coordinated/integrated ad campaign against the news with the company's marketing manager as the lead responsibility. The company tasked the Marketing manager to submit a proposal detailing the proposed strategies and cost-benefit analysis within five days. Prior to the next meeting, the Marketing manager had circulated the proposal to all members of the Management team. Convinced of all proposed strategies and recommendations, the Chairman of the company gave instructions to the Accountant for immediate release of the sum of N12,000,000 being the fund proposed for a three-month ad campaign on TV, radio and select social media platforms. In the course of the meeting, the Accountant informed that the company had already exhausted provisions for advertisement for the year and there was no available fund until the following year. He later advised that the company could source money through bank loan at a 25% annual compound interest rate if it was such an emergency. After a protracted deliberation, the Chairman came to the conclusion that, of the N12,500,000 Reserve capital, the sum of N12,000,000 be withdrawn for the proposed ad campaign.

CHAPTER TWELVE

Like soccer, businesses or any other life's endeavours should be guided by rules if there must be growth, progress, improved performance and profitability. The reasons why 90% of new startups fail, 75% of venture-backed startups fail, under 50% of businesses make it to their fifth year and only 40% of startups actually turn a profit, is because certain rules are not strictly adhered to. These rules had been explicitly discussed in the earlier chapters. However, they shall be summarized as follows:

➢ **Rule of Fit** – Any and every business is a subset of the entire global market, hence, it fits into it perfectly. No matter what you do, your business is only a dot in a big, circular world market. You can therefore take a any spot within the market and fit in perfectly.

➢ **Rule of Replacement** – An additional 20% of the business capital should be retained as security against capital or unforeseen business contingencies.

➢ **Rule of Fair Play** – Today's market place/space demands that an entrepreneur imbibes the fundamental values of fair play in order to succeed. Precisely, he must maintain effective relationship with his customers and also allow the relationship to sell his product or service.

➢ **Rule of Reward** – Performing teams in business deserve to be rewarded for their excellent performance. It is one thing to pay them salaries/wages or other compensations for doing the job, and another thing to pay them for a job well done. The latter is very important boosting and sustaining high performance.

- **Rule of Timing** – Most of the time when teams fail to get things done it is not because they cannot really get them done; it is because there is no commitment to get them done. If you are really serious about getting anything done, set a target for the activity and more importantly, set timing for carrying it out.
- **Rule of Recess** – Managers who want to see improvement in performance should be more employee-oriented in their approach. Meeting targets is good but meeting targets with no casualty and with every team player in high spirits is much better. Managers should learn to take a break and they should also encourage their teams to take breaks from work. This helps to reduce stress and fatigue and improve performance and output.
- **Rule of Training** – As it is possible for a soccer team with great individual talents to lose against a less talented but bonded team, so is it possible for an organization with highly skilled/qualified employees to perform poorly for lack of positive attitude, discipline and training.
- **Rule of Differentiation** – Entrepreneurs must constantly think of what they can do to differentiate their products or services from competition as there are competing brands fighting hard to become market leaders. If you sit back doing little or nothing to differentiate and position your brand favourably in the market place/space, your brand could be swallowed by better ones.
- **Rule of Penalty** – Penalties are used to moderate the activities of teams, departments/units and individuals within an organization in order to make them conform to set standards of operation, rules and norms. They are awarded to correct deviations in the organization.

- **Rule of Whistle Blowing** – Entrepreneurs are often caught in their own emotional web, a situation which causes them to take certain emotional decisions that are detrimental to the survival of the business. To ensure, therefore, that entrepreneurs play the business game according to the rule, a control measure, also known as whistle blowing, must be put in place.

Summary

CHAPTER THIRTEEN

CONCLUSION

Rules are important in business or any life's endeavours. Watch closely and consider any individual, business venture, family, society or nation that is successful. They are not just successful by chance; they are successful by rules. Even in a nuclear family that has a father as the head or any other member (in the absence of the father), there must be certain unwritten rules guiding them if they must succeed. if the head decides to care less about what any member does, such a family will not stand in the long run. A rule as simple as, "nobody must stay outside longer than 8:00PM" can be a life saver especially in a society that has a high rate of crime.

In business, rules must be strictly adhered to in order to engender growth and progress. Any attempt by a member of the team to flout established rules will both slow the pace of the team and of the business. Therefore, effort must be made by management of any business to ensure that every member of the team plays the game according to rules.

Also, in any nation, the arm of government that administers rules for all is the judiciary. When the judiciary is relegated to the background, what follows is failure. Justice and fair play are important ingredients to a sane, peaceful, progressive and prosperous society. When they are lost, chaos, civil unrest, lawlessness and anarchy will be the order of the day.

Finally, it is not just important to make rules, it is also very important to abide strictly by the rules.

IMAGE/HYPERTEXT INDEX

The World

https://www.pri.org/stories/2020-12-29/got-space-junk-wooden-satellites-may-be-solution Chapter 2, Page 11;

FIFA.com

https://twitter.com/FIFAcom?ref_src=twsrc%5Etfw%7Ctwcamp%5Etweetembed%7Ctwterm%5E1034798574041616384%7Ctwgr%5E%7Ctwcon%5Es1_&ref_url=https%3A%2F%2Fdailyactive.info%2F2018%2F08%2F29%2Ffifas-new-fifth-substitute-rule%2F Chapter 3, Page 17;

MasterFile

https://www.masterfile.com/search/en/fair+play+football Chapter 4, Page 23;

Premier Skills English

https://premierskillsenglish.britishcouncil.org/skills/listen/week/cup-finals-wins-liverpool-chelsea Chapter 5, Page 37;

ScoreVision

https://scorevision.com/our-software/scoreboard/soccer/ Chapter 6, Page 43;

E&E News

https://www.google.com/imgres?imgurl=https%3A%2F%2Fwww.eenews.net%2Fimage_assets%2F2019%2F07%2Fimage_asset_57191.jpg&imgrefurl=https%3A%2F%2Fwww.eenews.net%2Fstories%2F1060683061&tbnid=Zn843RpPL5ZqeM&vet=12ahUKEwiDvOv5iIjwAhX1gM4BHZcyBJsQMyg6egQIARBJ..i&docid=xKTKL_0iRTq3kM&w=938&h=483&q=image%20of%20break%20in%20soccer&ved=2ahUKEwiDvOv5iIjwAhX1gM4BHZcyBJsQMyg6egQIARBJ Chapter 7, Page 47;

WikiMedia Commons
https://commons.wikimedia.org/wiki/File:Brazil_national_football_team_training_at_Dobsonville_Stadium_2010-06-03_13.jpg Chapter 8, Page 53;

Liverpool FC
https://www.google.com/imgres?imgurl=https%3A%2F%2Fd3j2s6hdd6a7rg.cloudfront.net%2Fv2%2Fuploads%2Fmedia%2Fdefault%2F0001%2F74%2Fthumb_73187_default_news_size_5.jpeg&imgrefurl=https%3A%2F%2Fwww.liverpoolfc.com%2Fnews%2Ffirst-team%2F318302-match-report-liverpool-chelsea-carabao-cup&tbnid=9s6CFe1xAnSa3M&vet=12ahUKEwjjr_KHkojwAhVEdBoKHcTqDhEQMygFegUIARDFAQ..i&docid=SH1G7x8vK_Q7SM&w=850&h=510&q=LIVERPOOL%20FC%20AND%20CHELSEA%20BEFORE%20THE%20MATCH&ved=2ahUKEwjjr_KHkojwAhVEdBoKHcTqDhEQMygFegUIARDFAQ Chapter 9, Page 57;

Sportskeeda
https://www.google.com/imgres?imgurl=https%3A%2F%2Fstaticg.sportskeeda.com%2Fwp-content%2Fuploads%2F2015%2F03%2Fbayern-vs-chelsea-penalty-1427546112.jpg&imgrefurl=https%3A%2F%2Fwww.sportskeeda.com%2Ffootball%2Fthe-history-of-penalties-and-penalty-shoot-outs&tbnid=jWw3d8bsRSc40M&vet=12ahUKEwim_ZLlk4jwAhVKnRoKHS1RBZoQMygMegUIARDrAQ..i&docid=c8AmPJI_QA-GzM&w=660&h=387&q=penalty%20kick&ved=2ahUKEwim_ZLlk4jwAhVKnRoKHS1RBZoQMygMegUIARDrAQ Chapter 10, Page 63;

BreakingViews
https://www.breakingviews.com/considered-view/us-well-placed-to-blow-whistle-on-soccer-excess/ Chapter 11, Page 69.

NOTE

www.ingramcontent.com/pod-product-compliance
Lightning Source LLC
Chambersburg PA
CBHW070455220526
45466CB00004B/1832